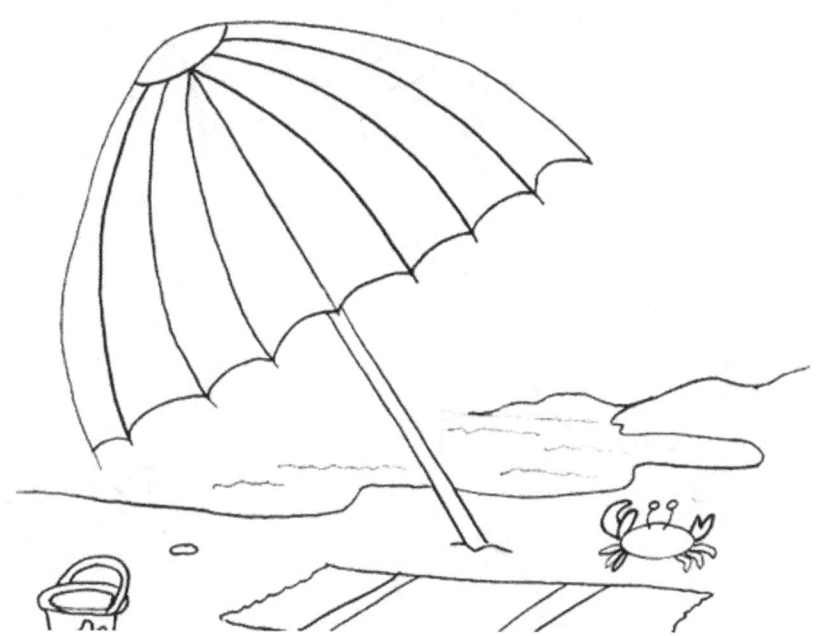

There is something about summer that just brings the life out of us, isn't there? Well, those sun-filled, warm-breeze days are here with us yet again (thank goodness) and of course you will be looking for fun summer activities and things to do.

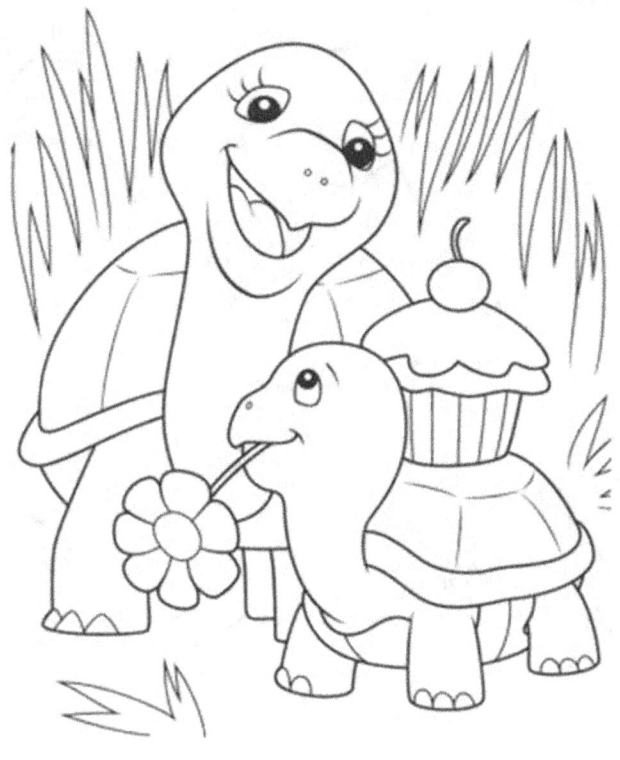

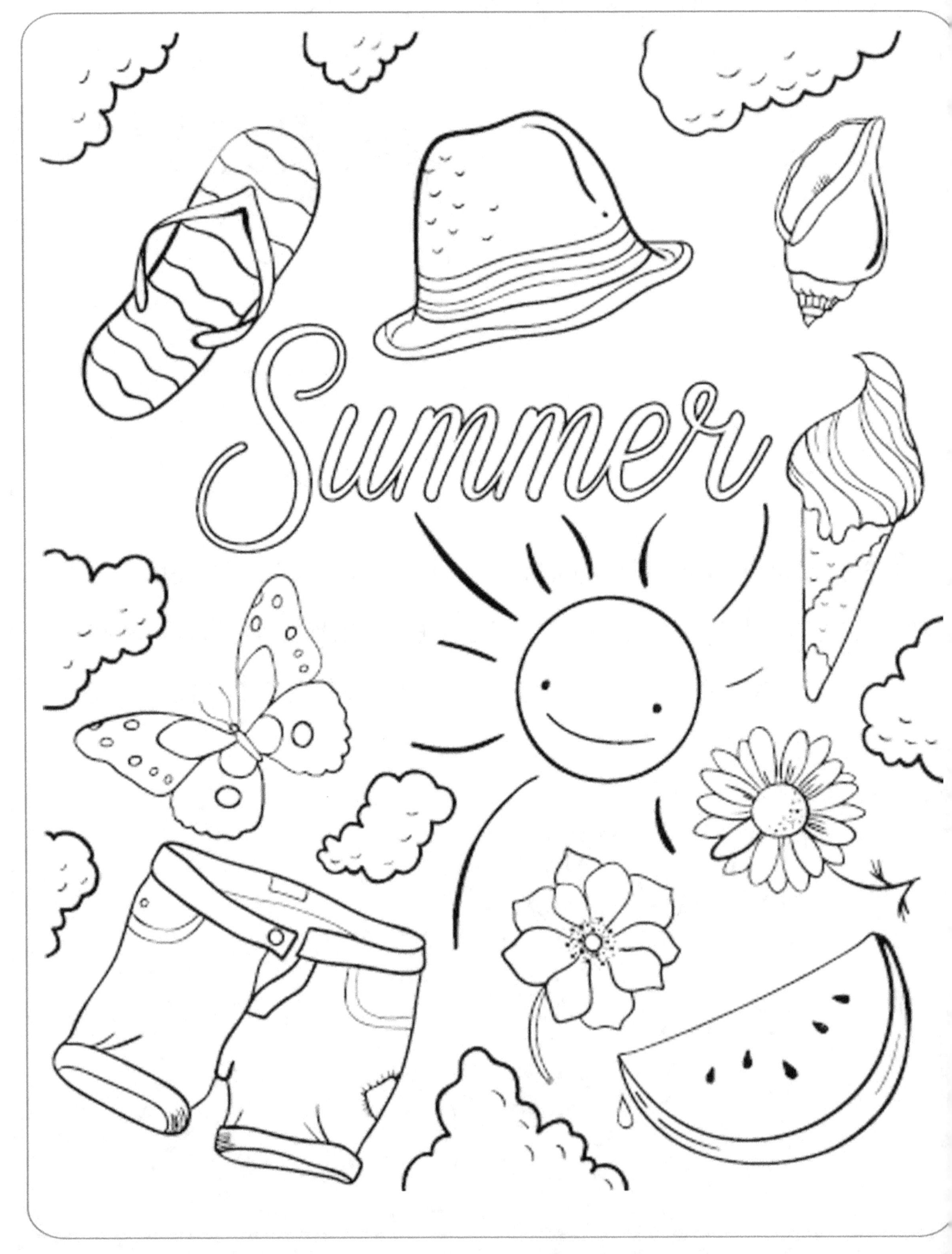

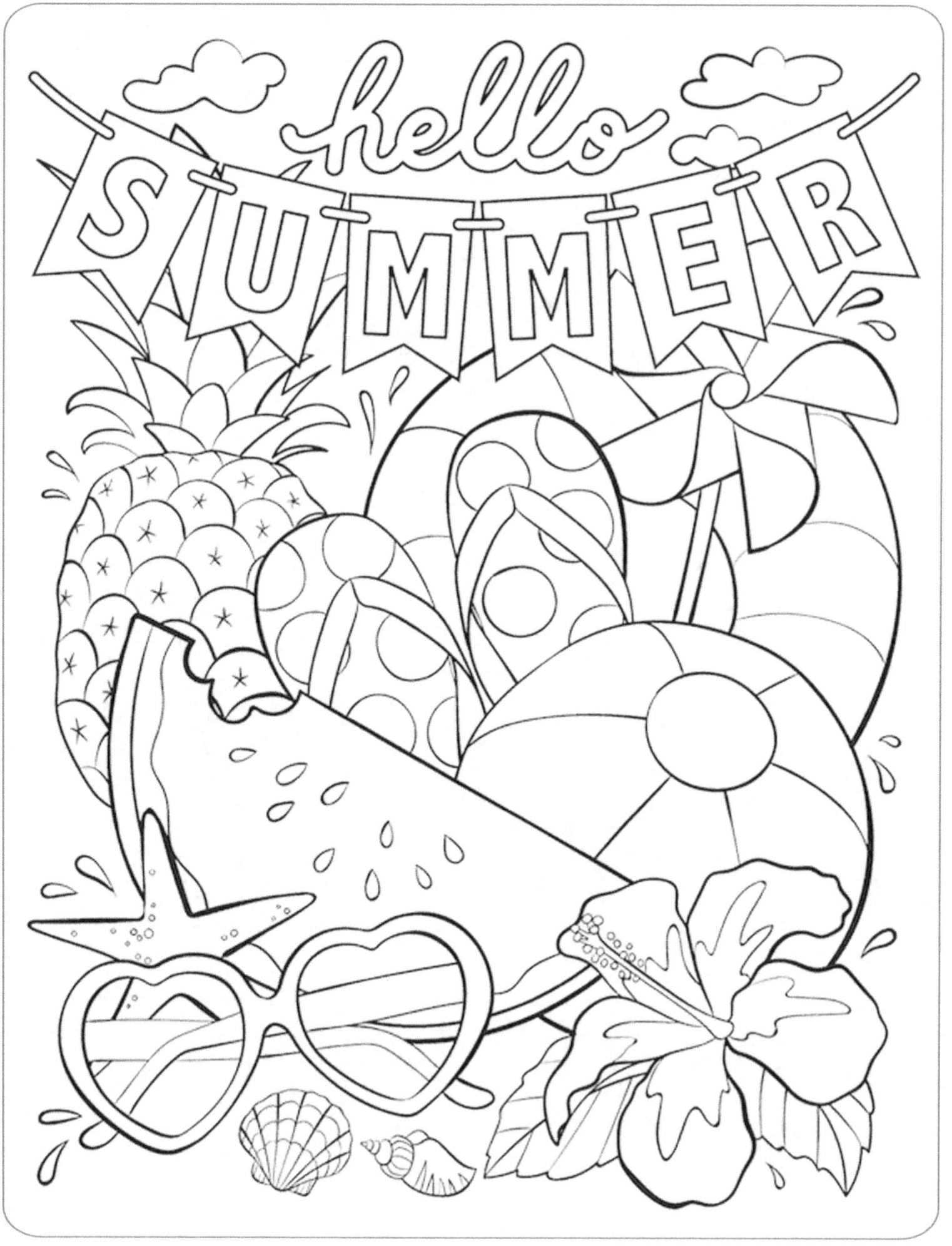

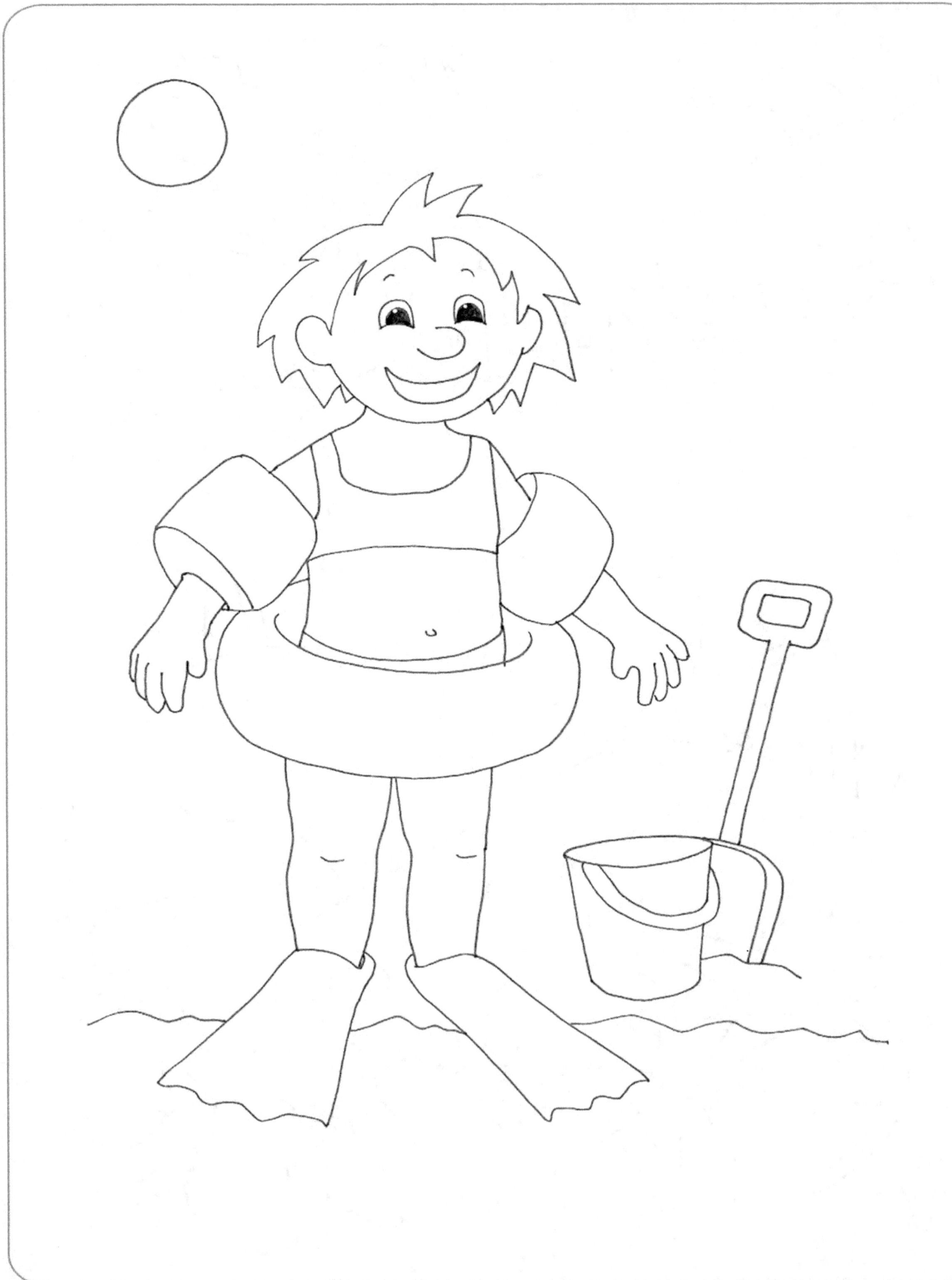

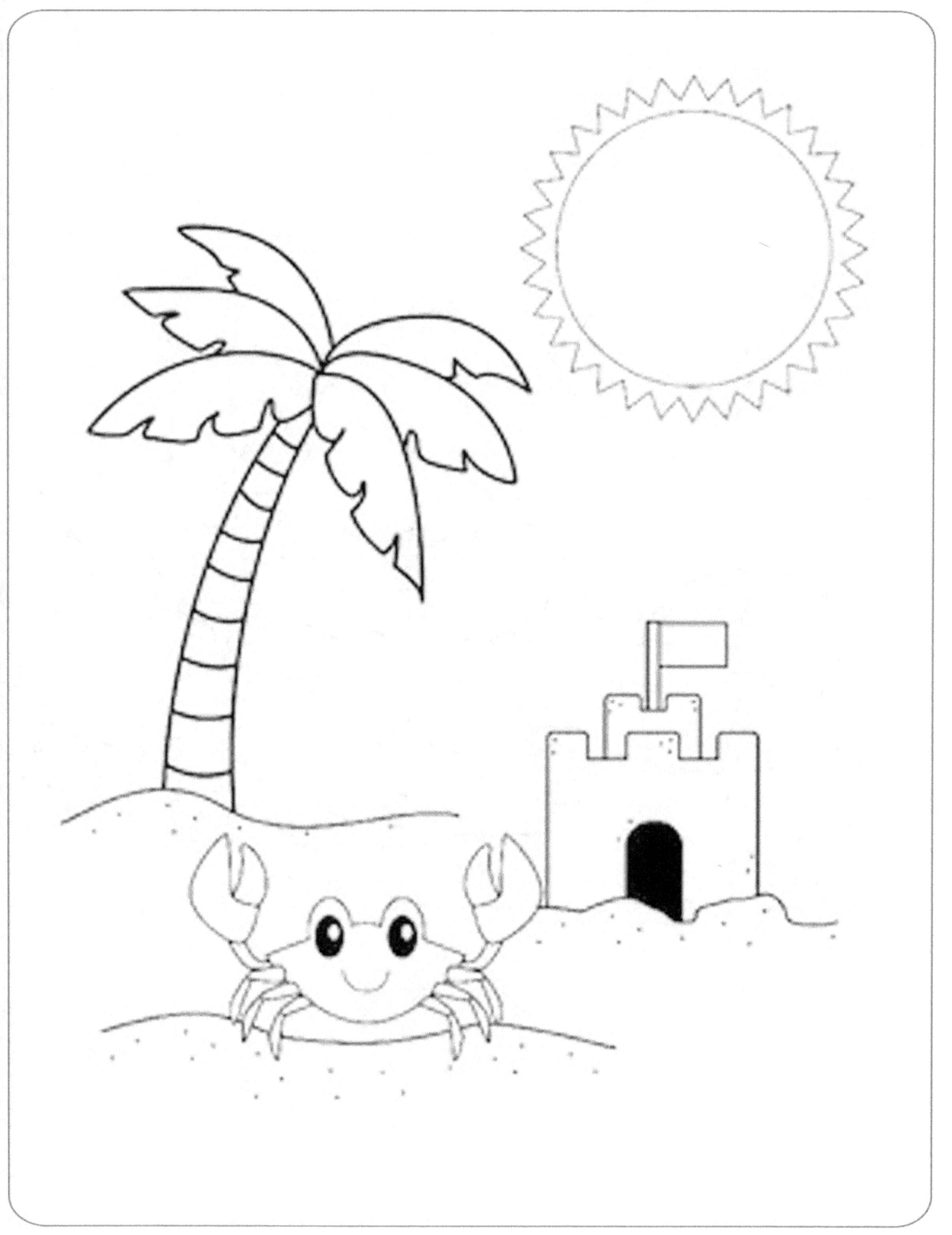

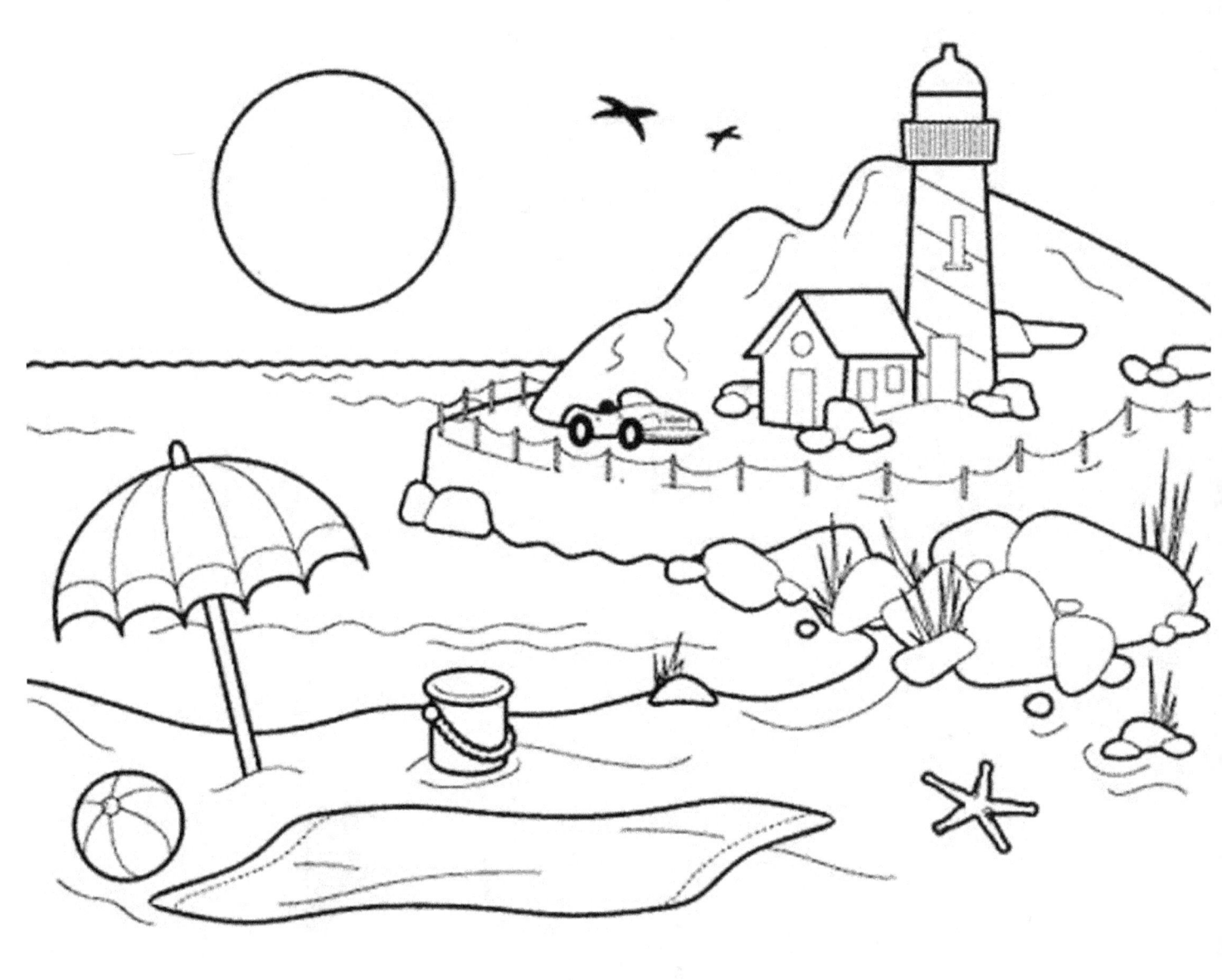

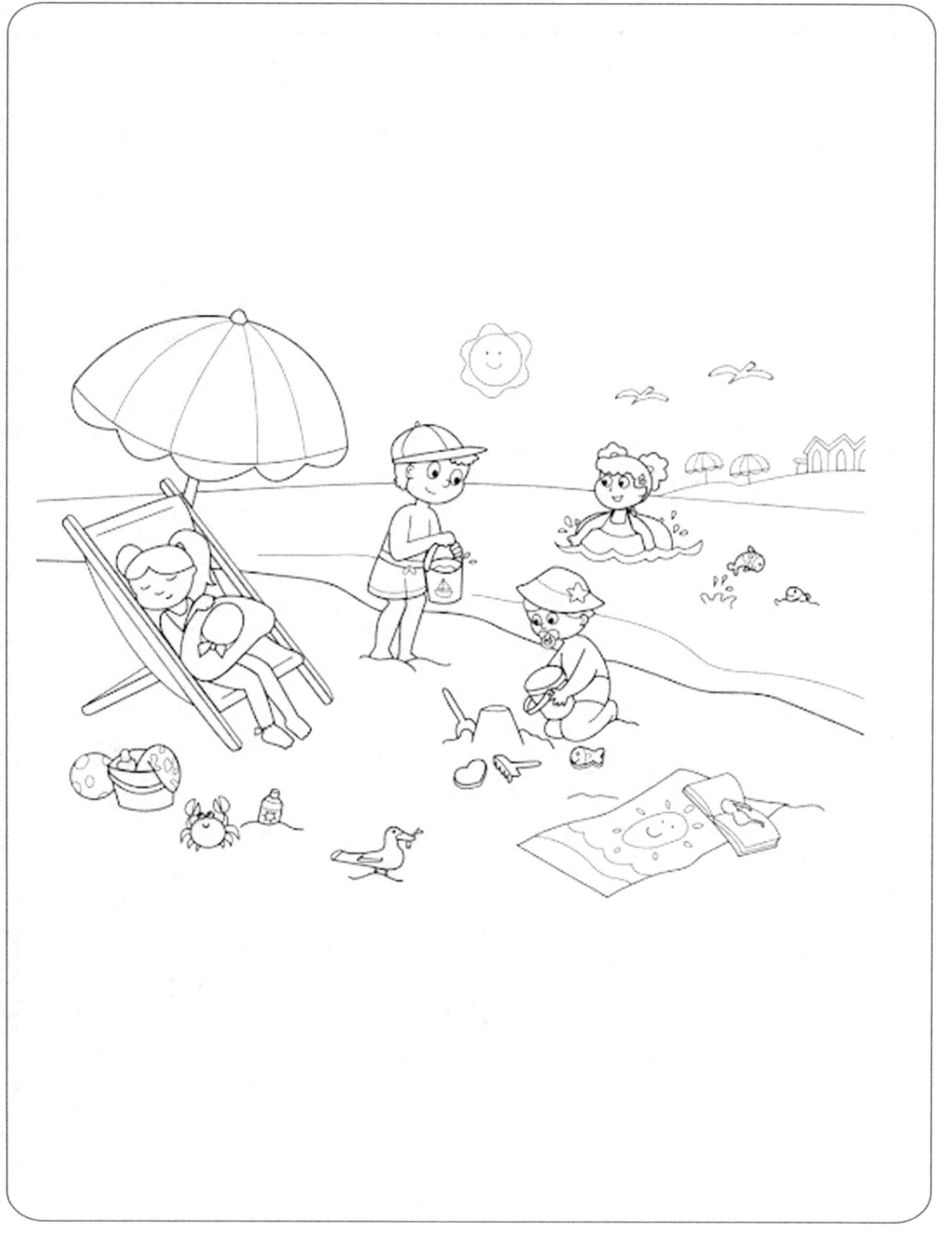

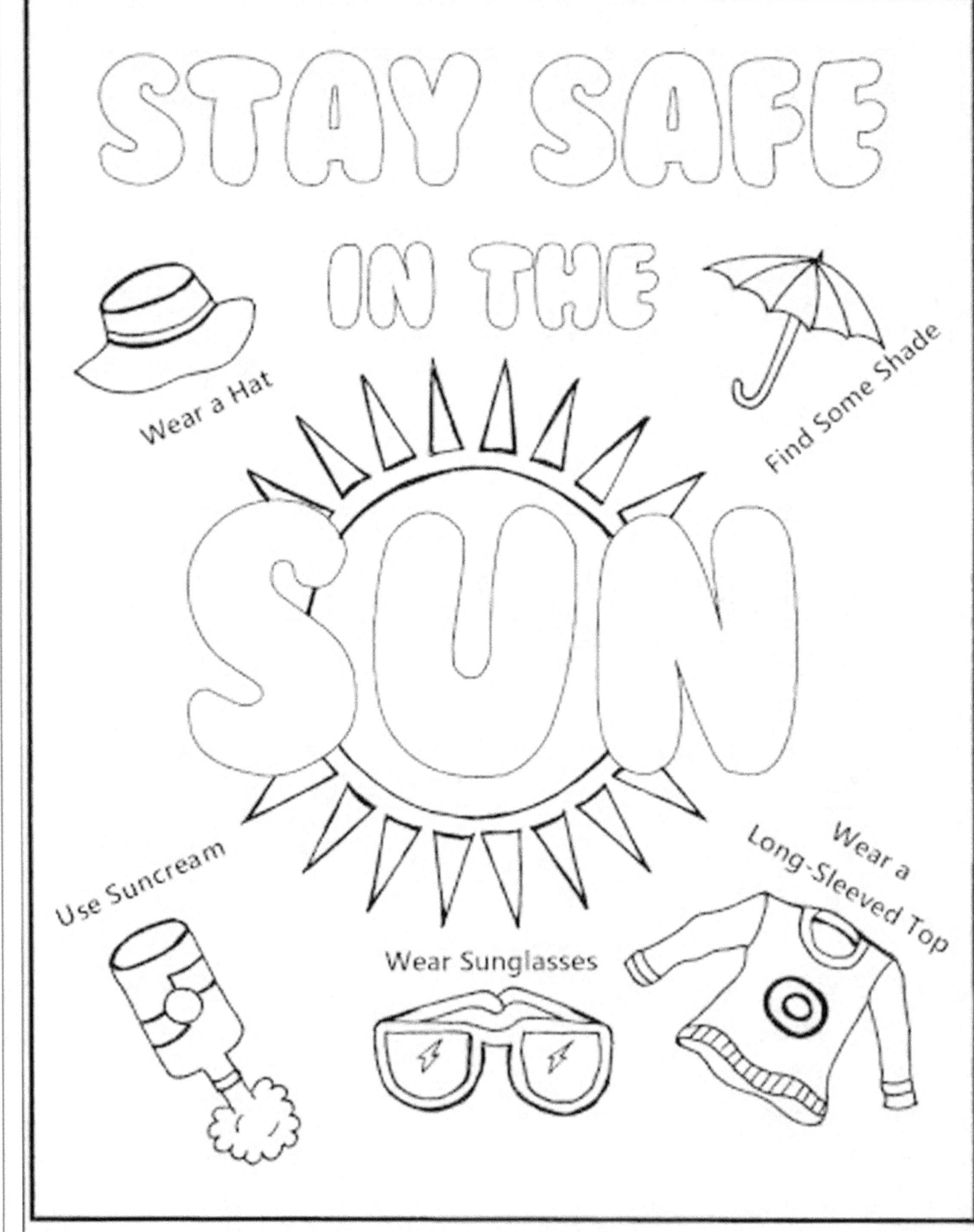

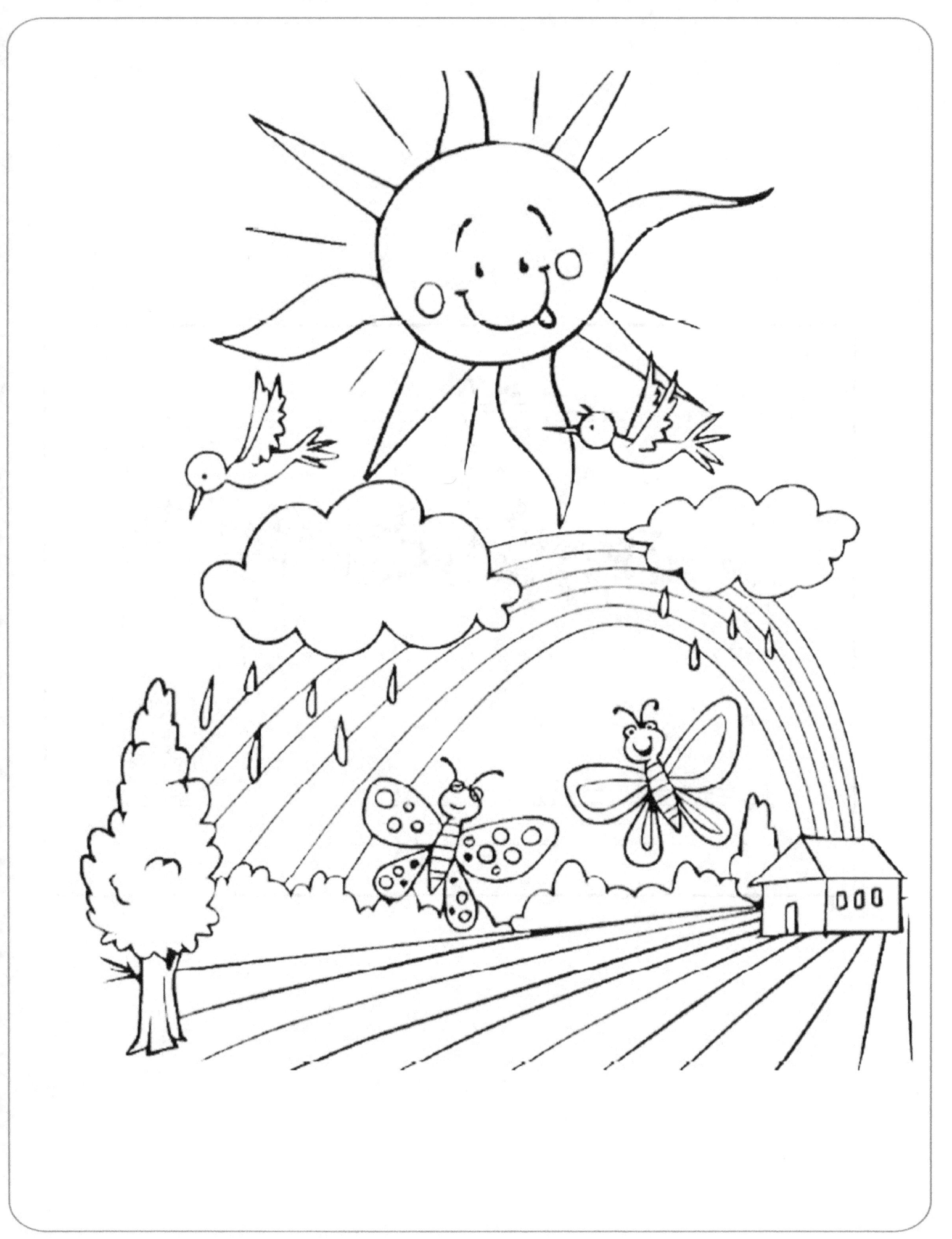

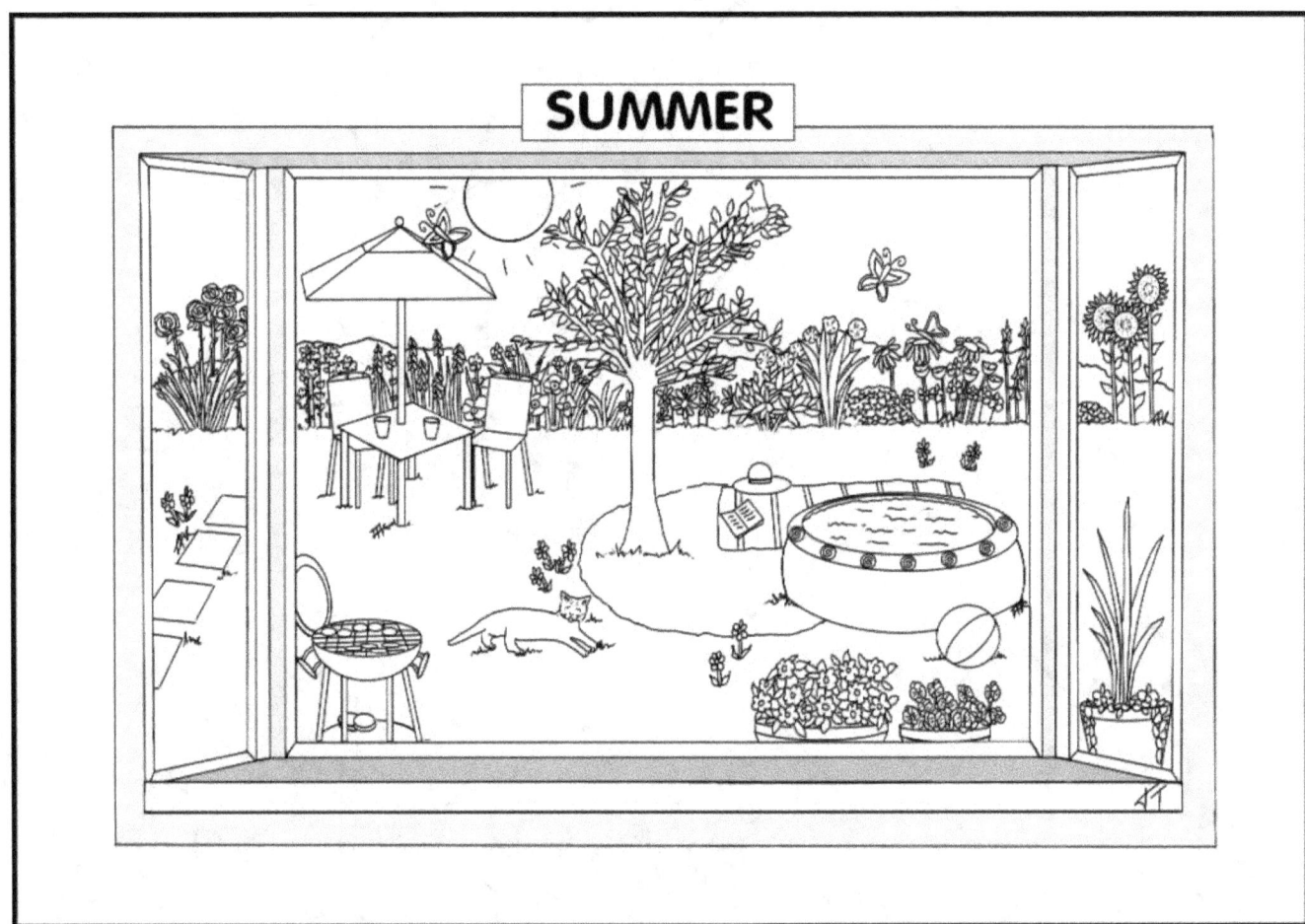

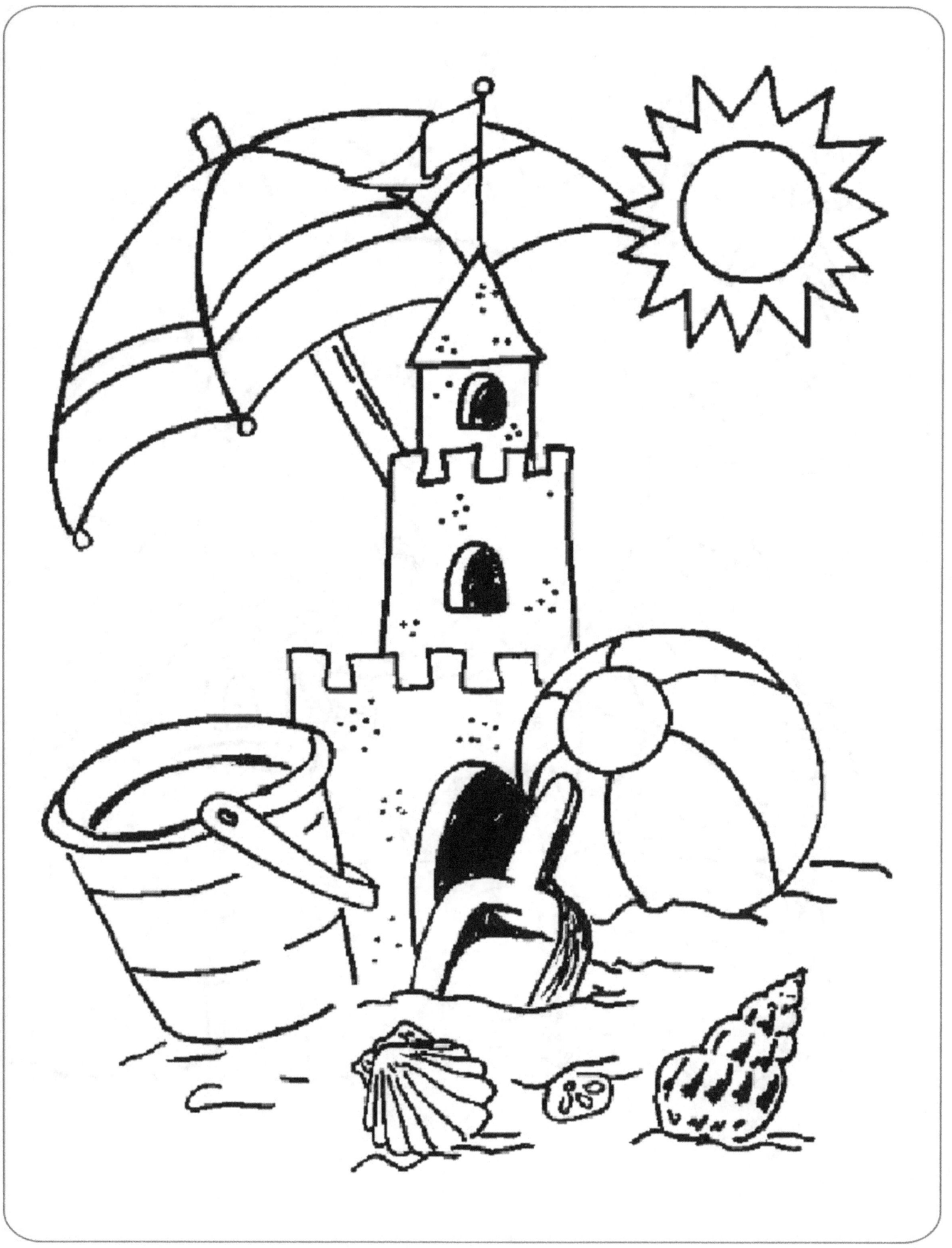

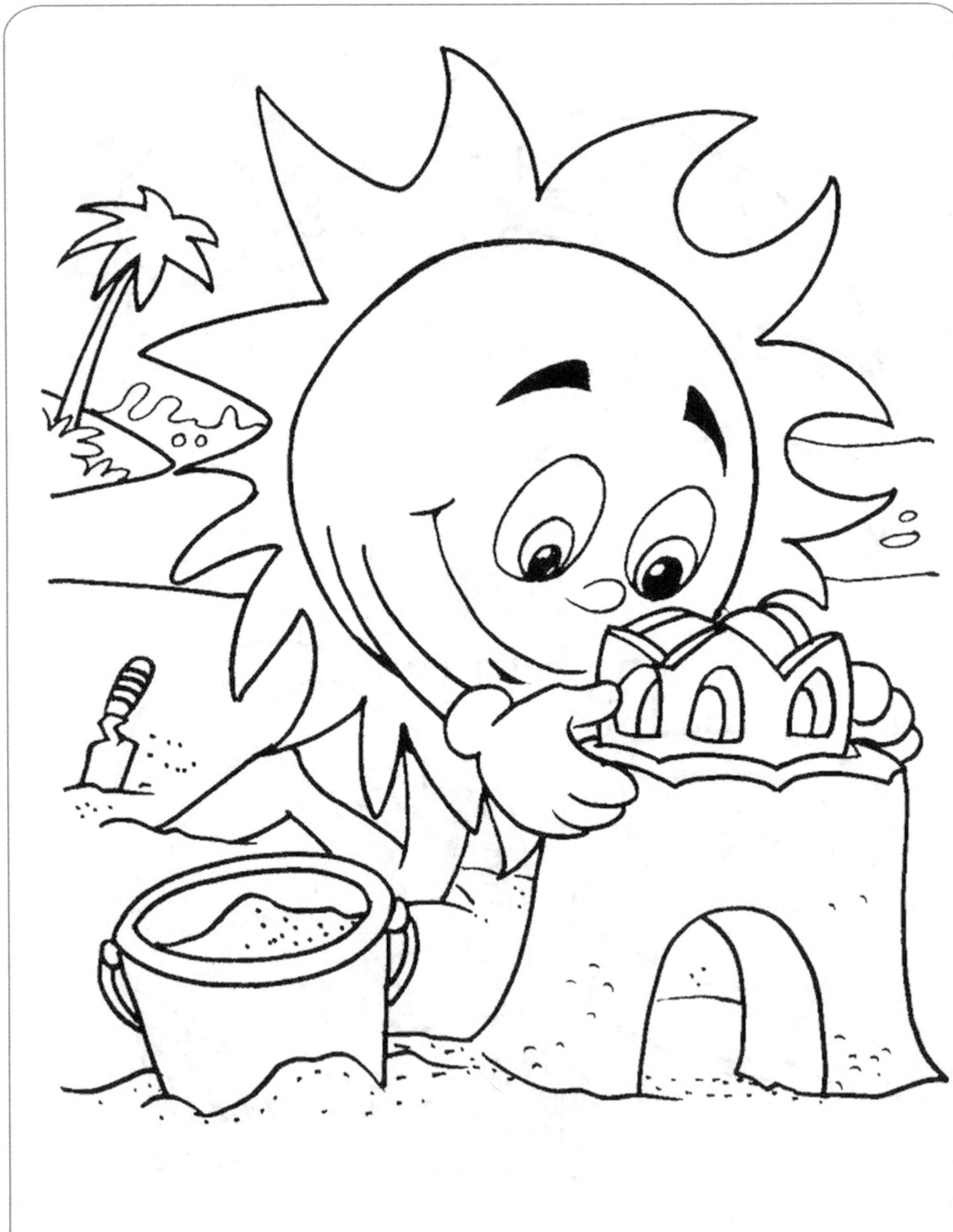

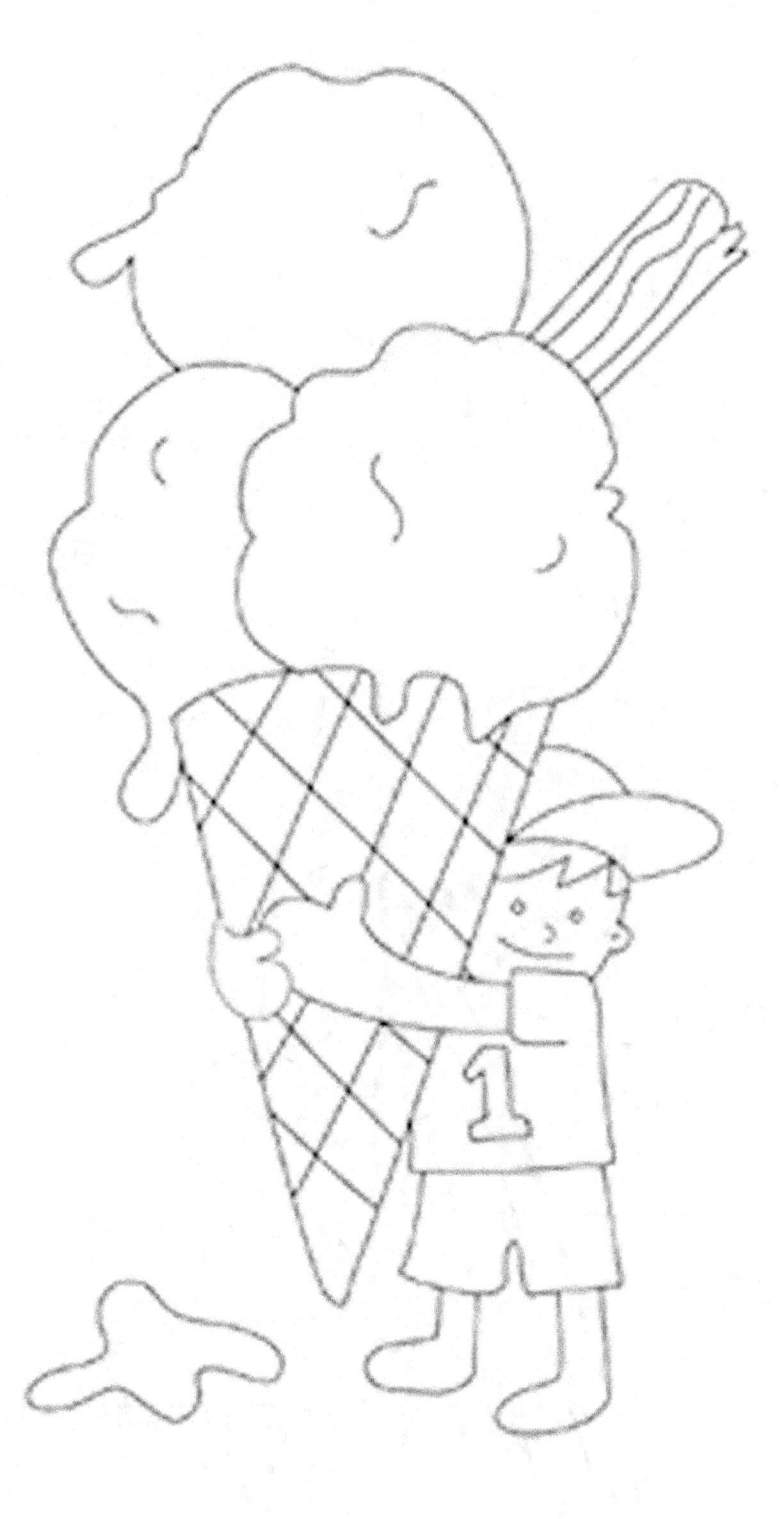

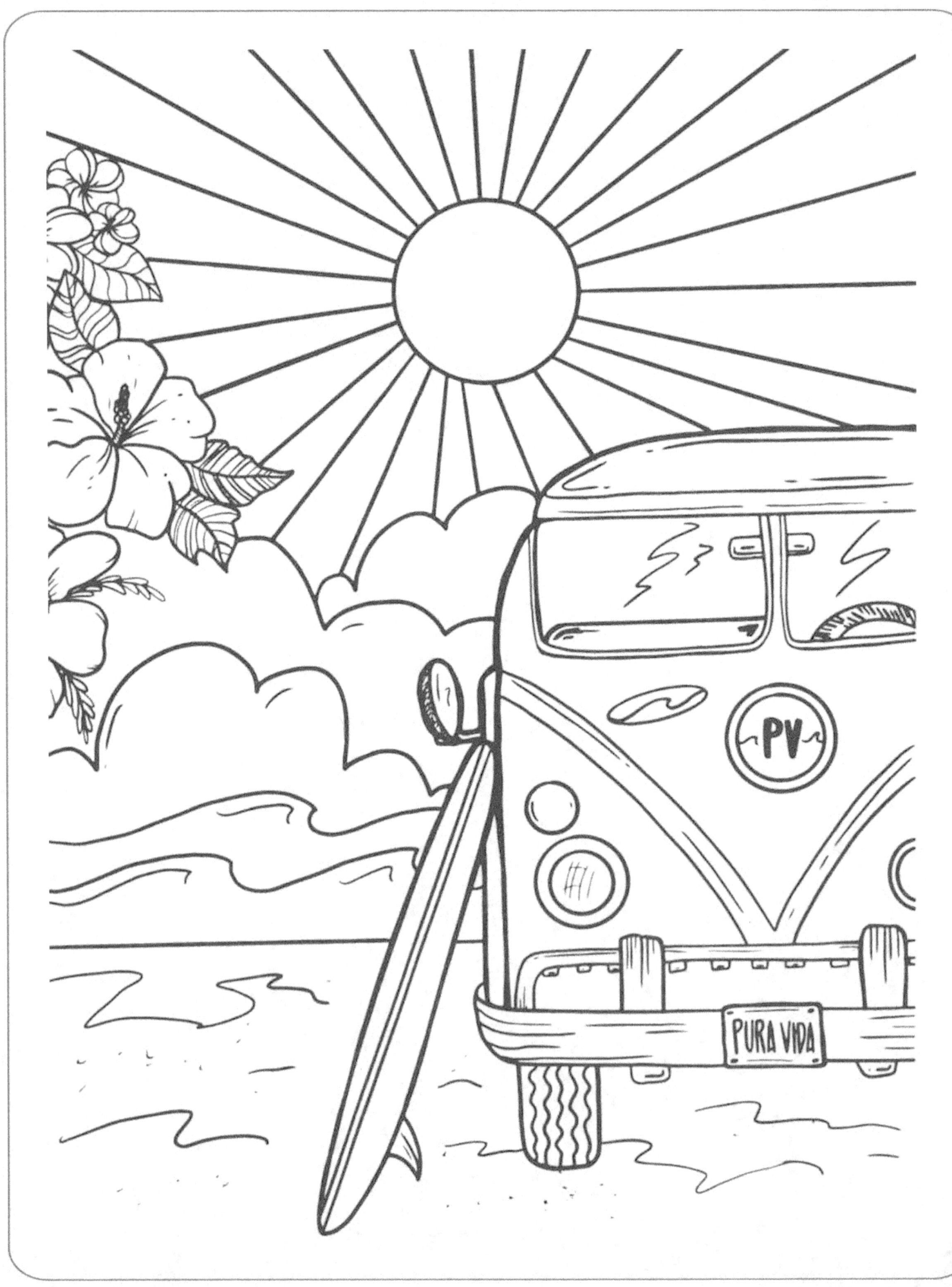

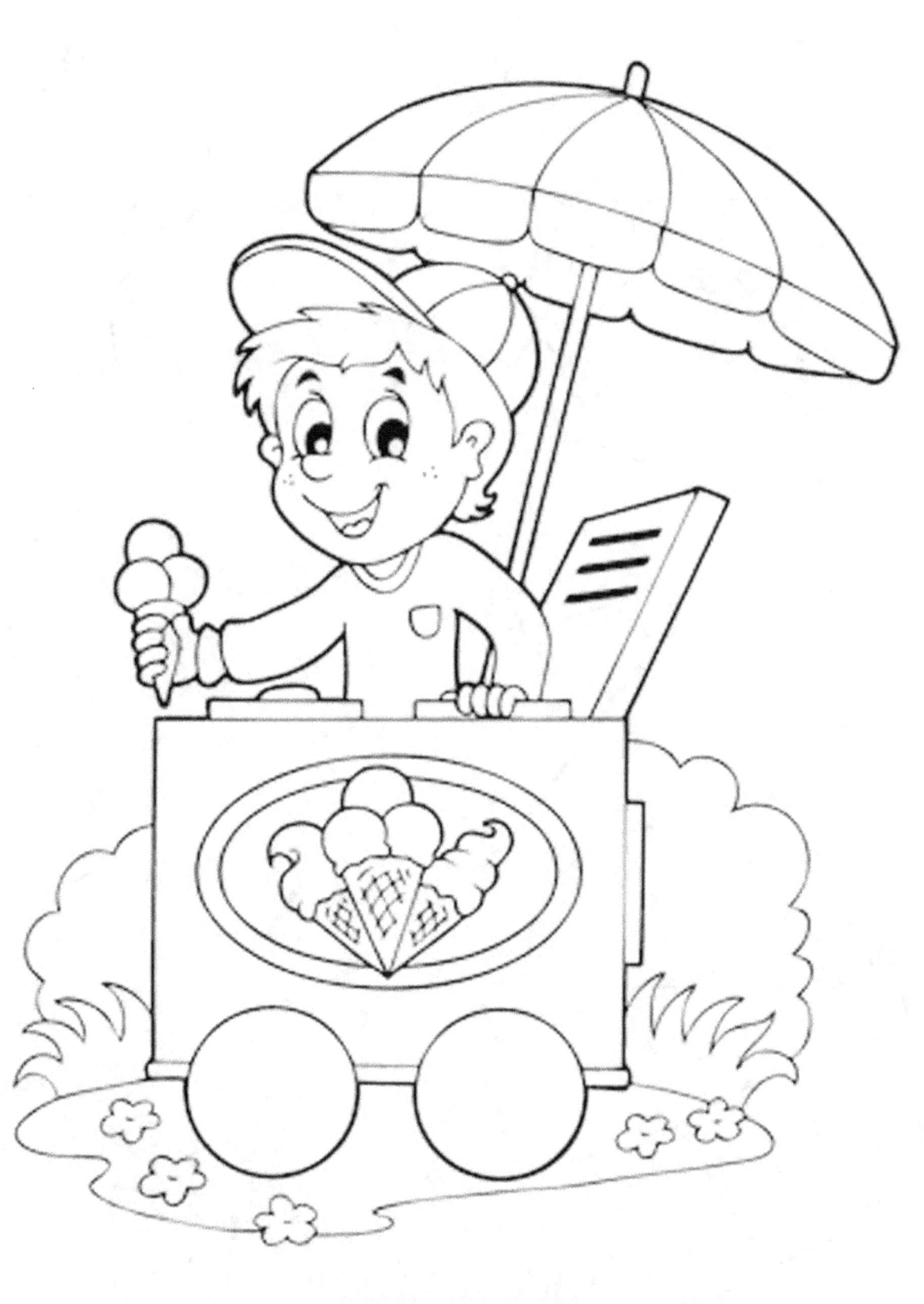

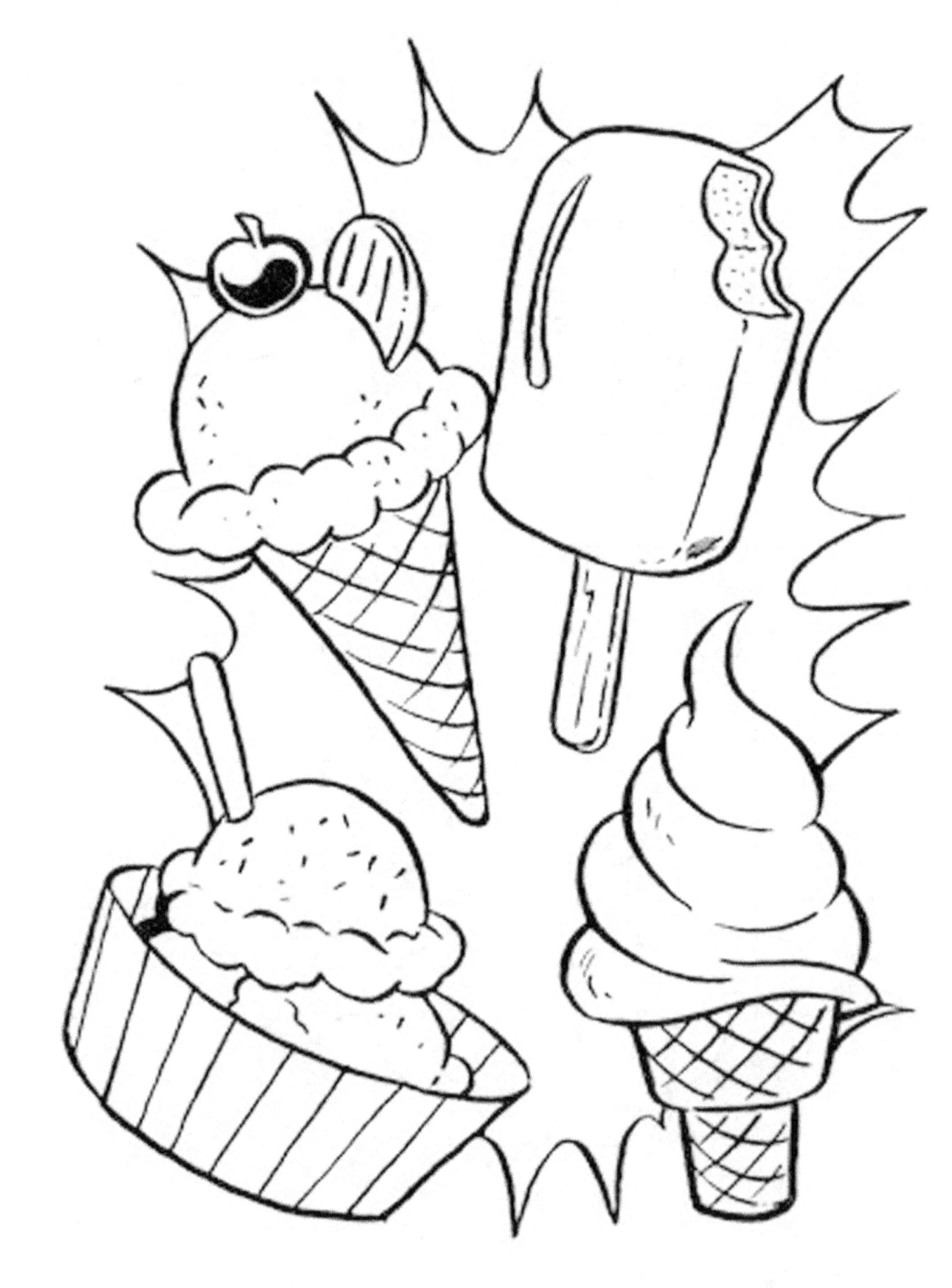

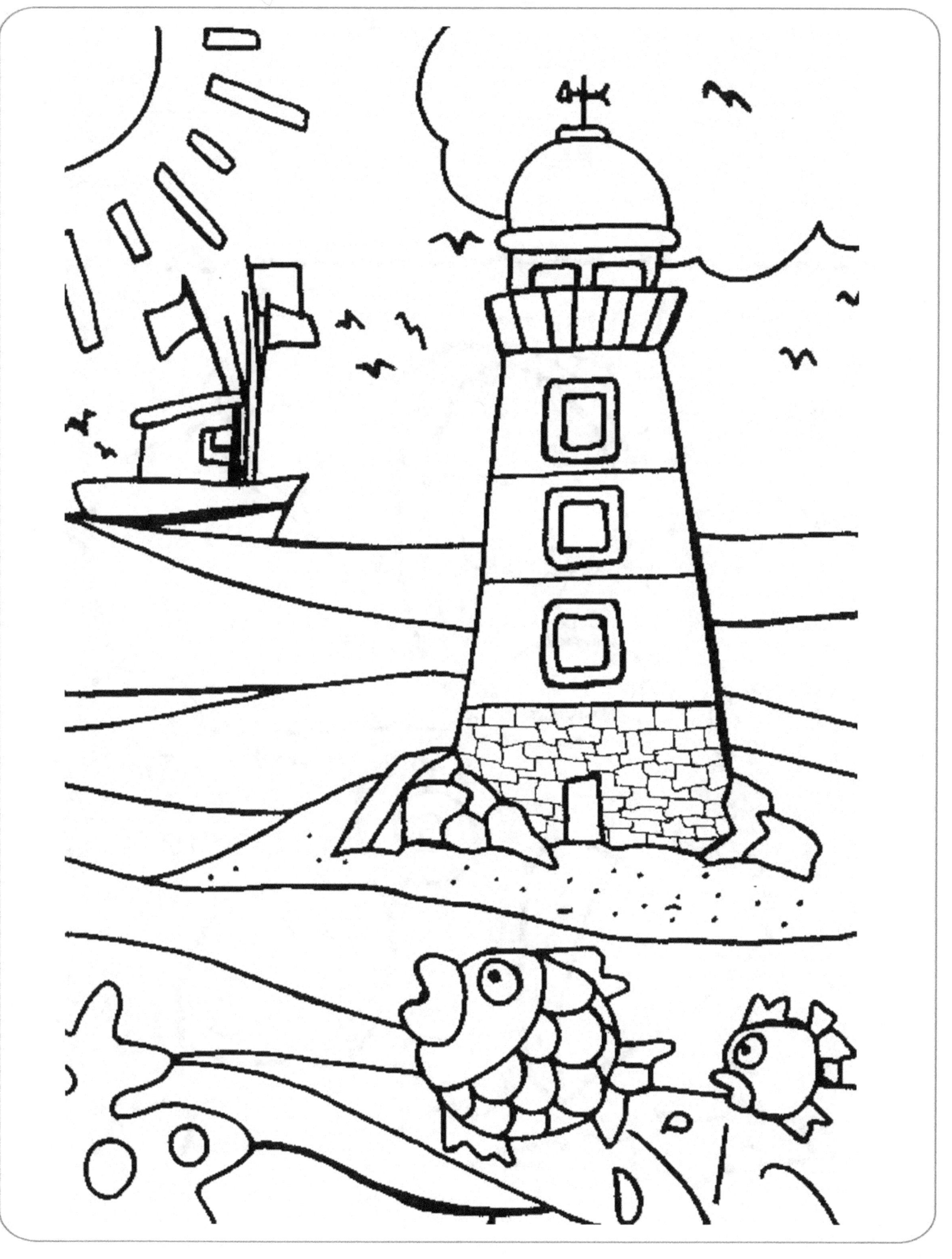

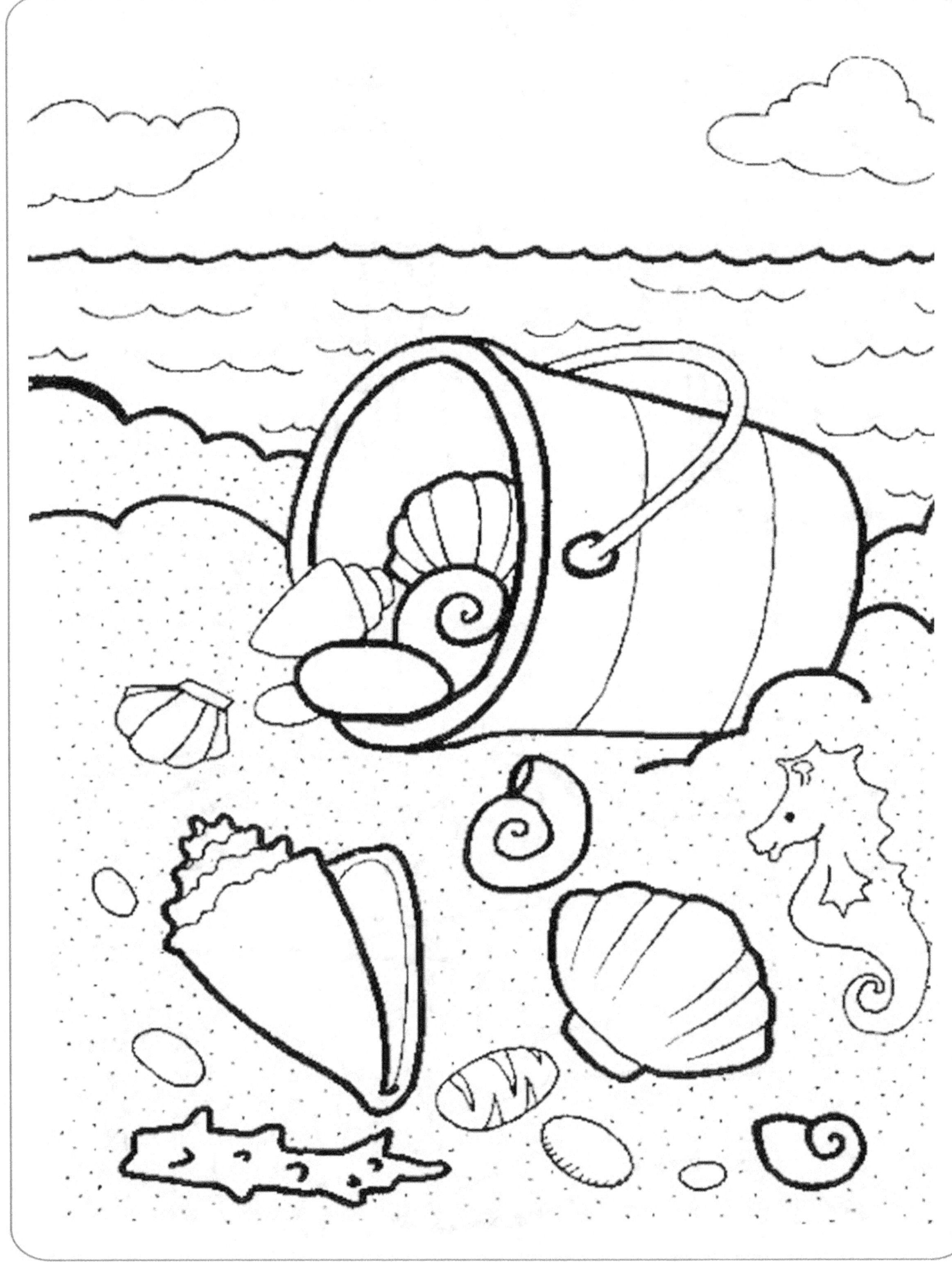

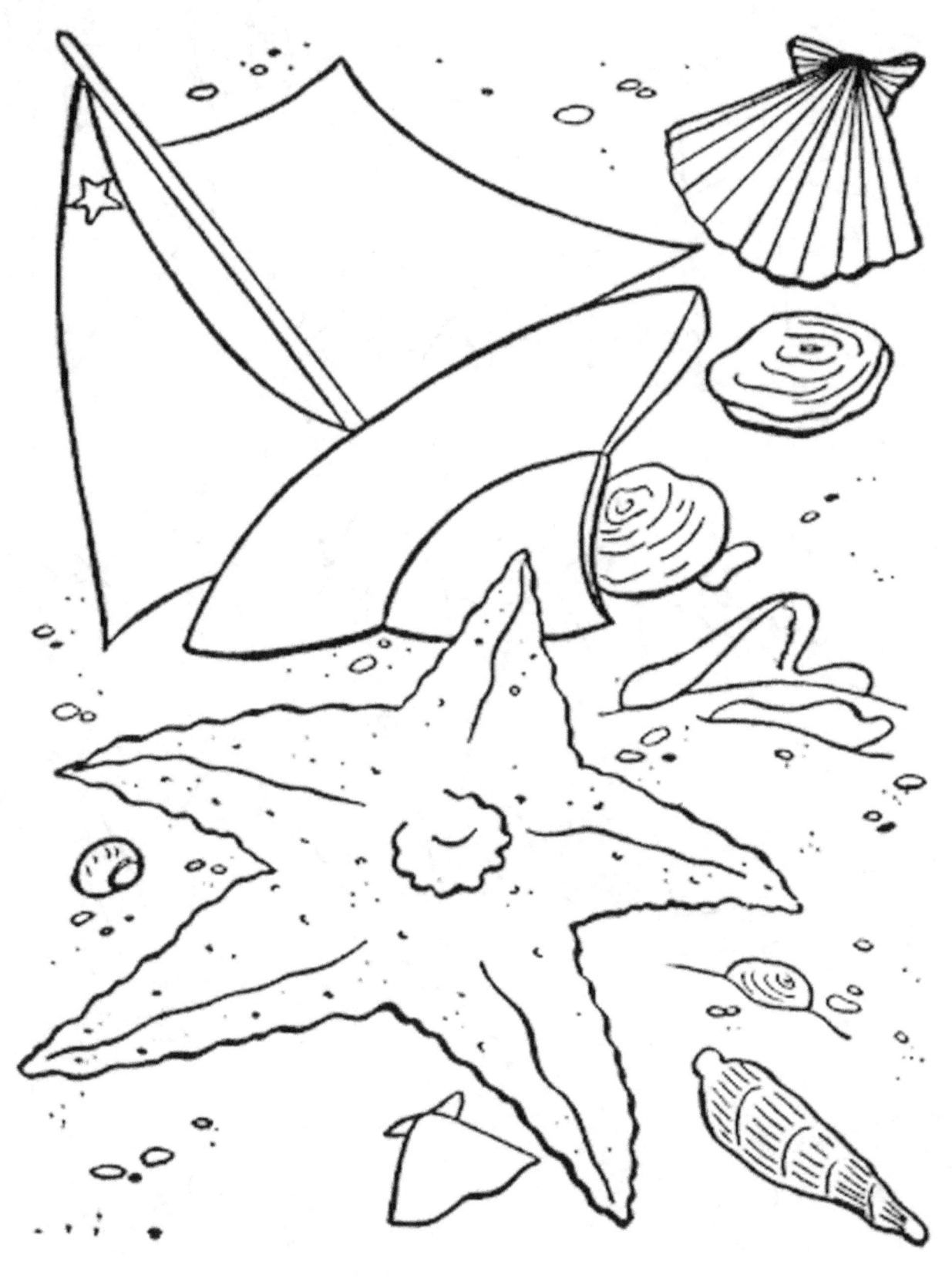

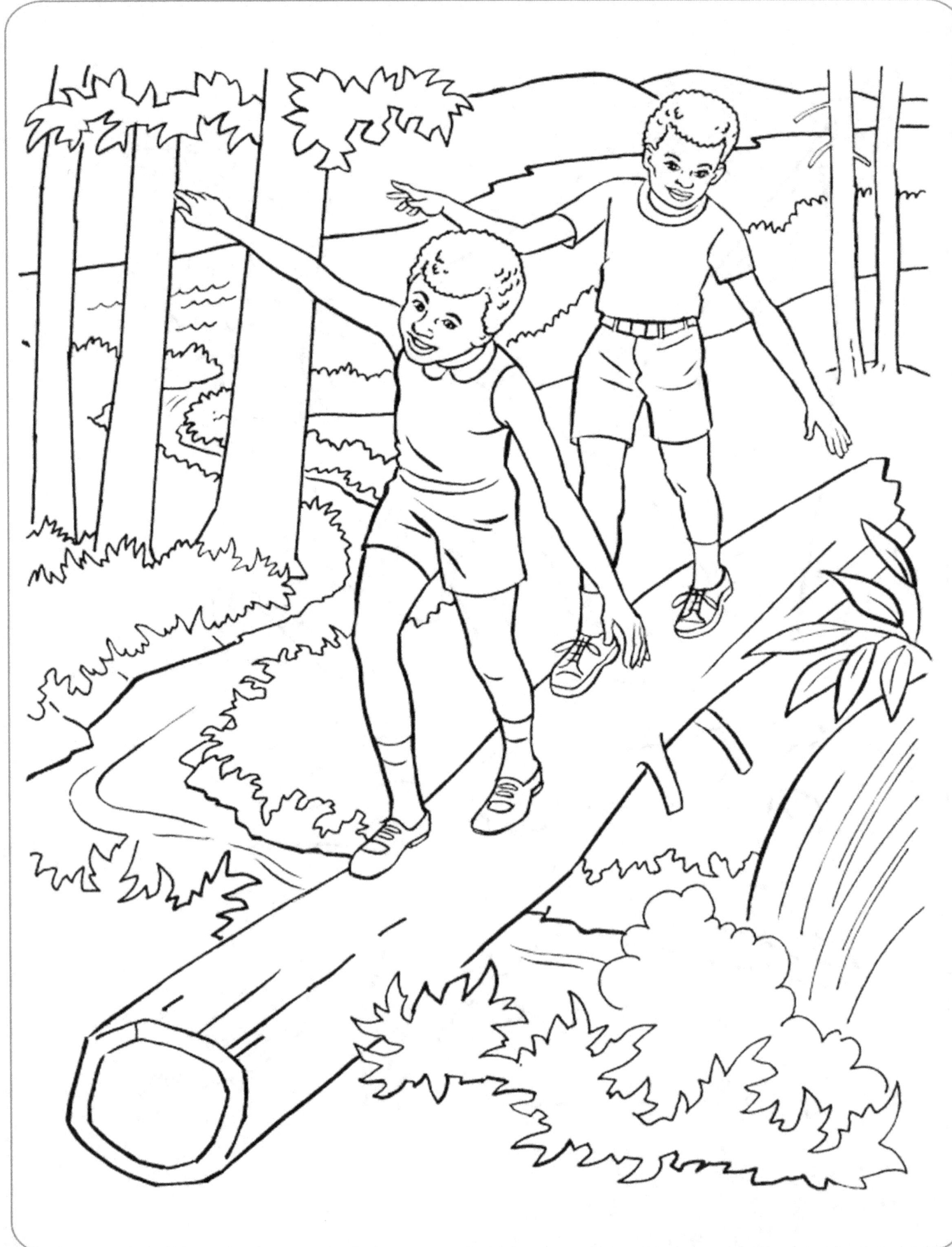

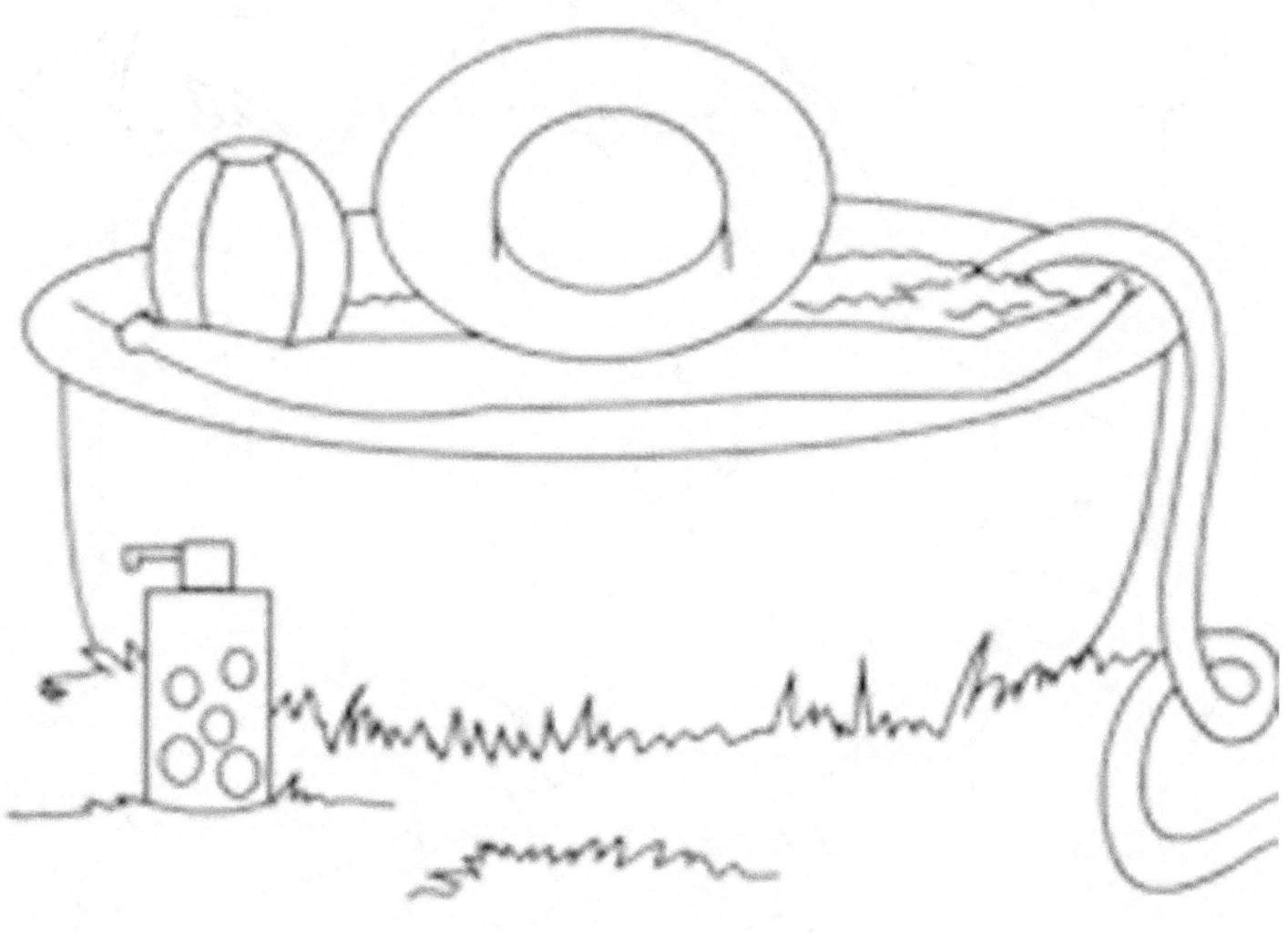

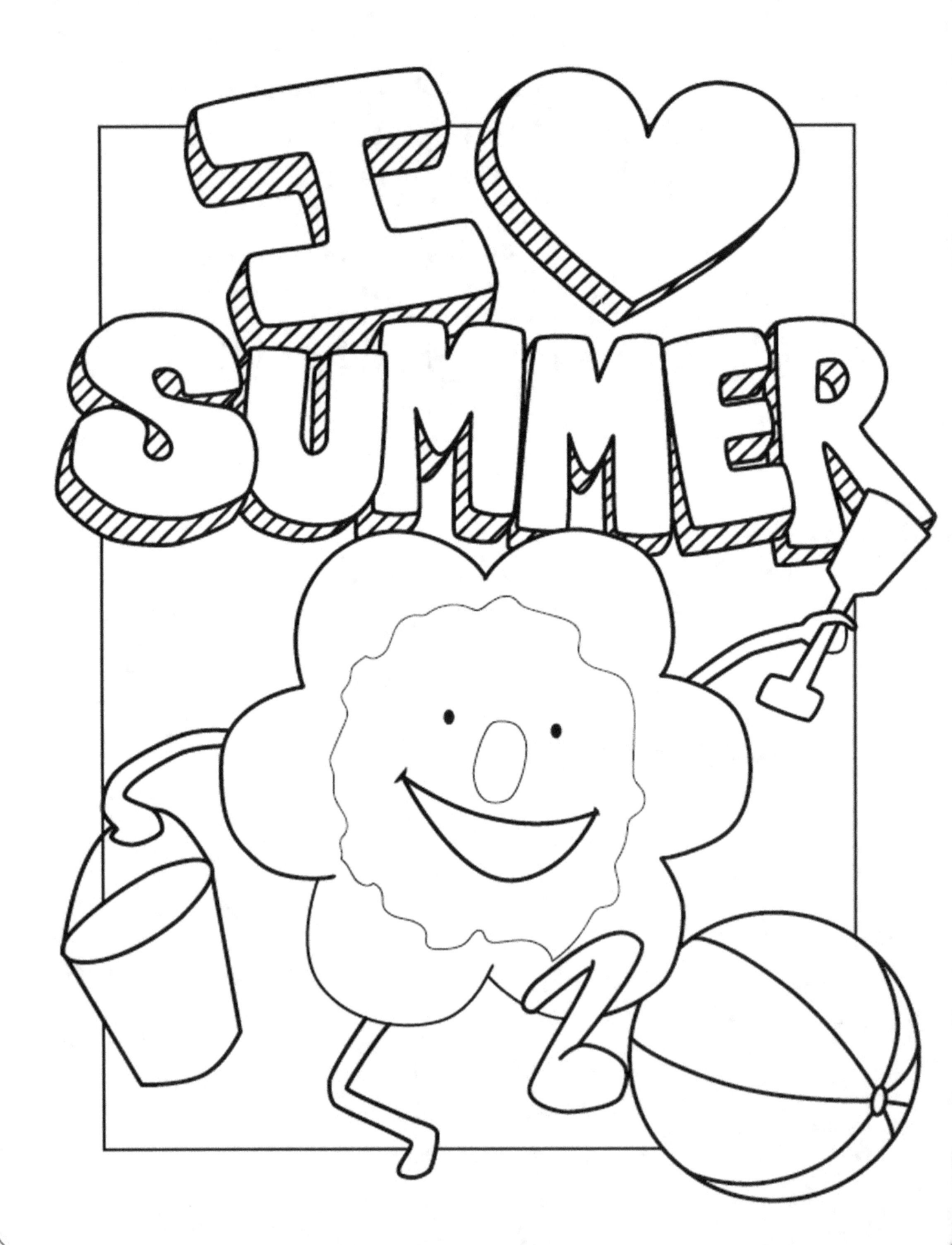

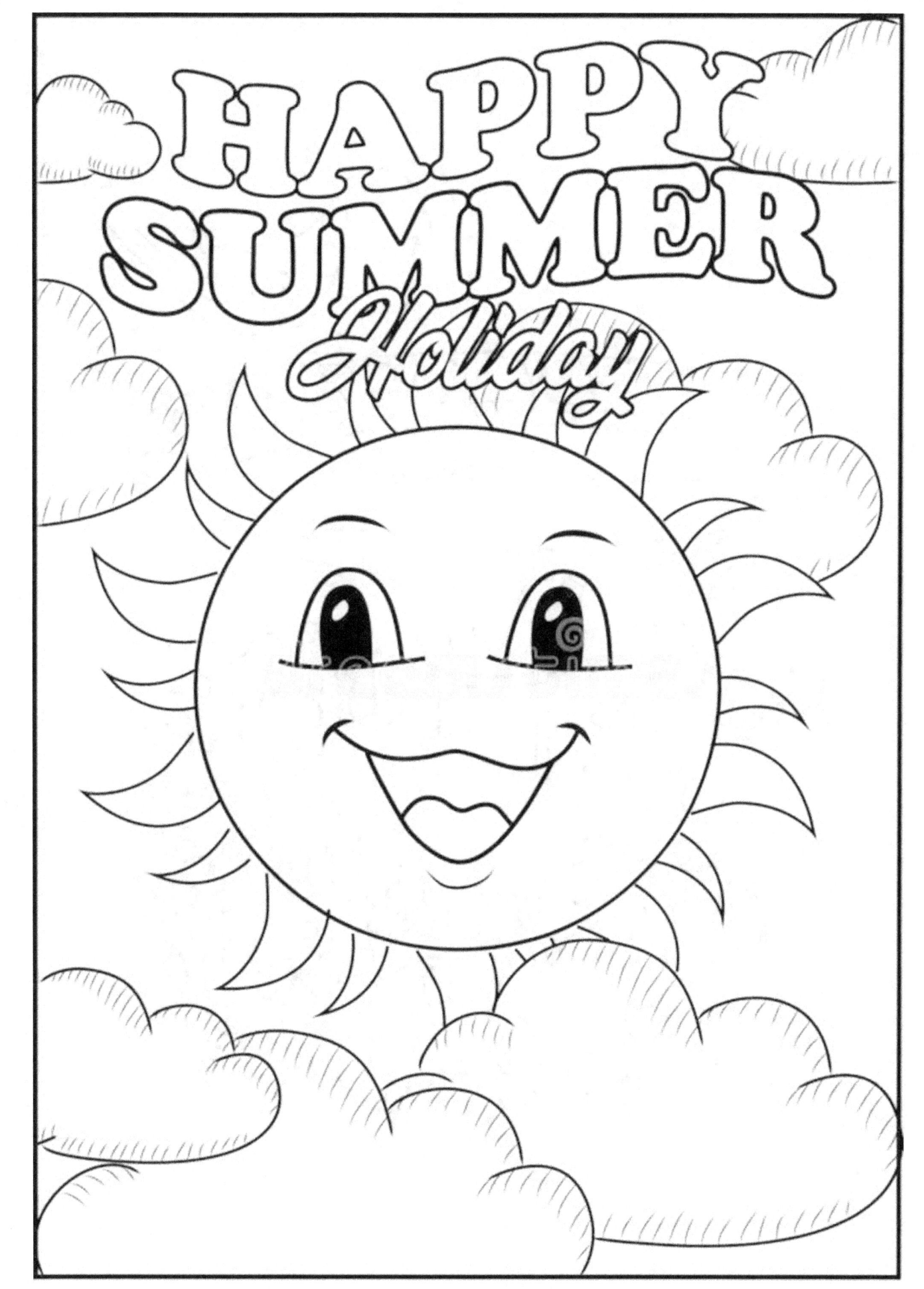

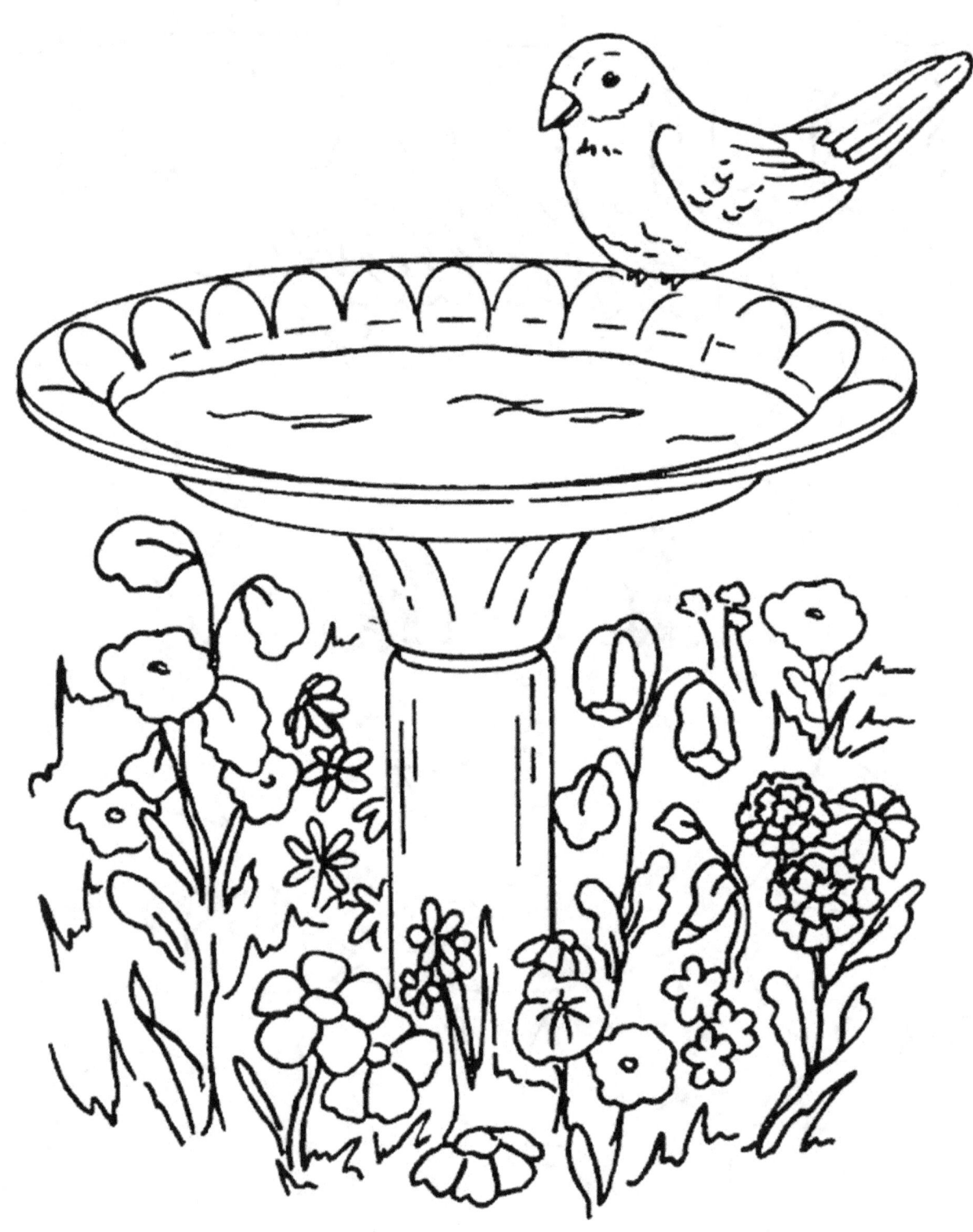

www.ingramcontent.com/pod-product-compliance
Lightning Source LLC
Chambersburg PA
CBHW080821220526
45466CB00011BB/3645